101 THINGS

YOU NEVER KNEW ABOUT
DISNEYLAND

D0374228

101 THINGS
YOU NEVER KNEW ABOUT DISNEYLAND

An Unauthorized Look at the Little Touches and Inside Jokes

Kevin Yee and Jason Schultz

Zauberreich Press
Orlando, Florida

101 Things You Never Knew About Disneyland: An Unauthorized
Look at the Little Touches and Inside Jokes
by Kevin Yee and Jason Schultz

Published by
ZAUBERREICH PRESS

Cover design and illustrations by "The Dozak"

This book makes reference to various Disney copyrighted characters,
trademarks, marks, and registered marks owned by The Walt Disney
Company and Disney Enterprises, Inc.

101 Things You Never Knew About Disneyland is not endorsed by,
sponsored by, or connected with The Walt Disney Company and/or
Disney Enterprises, Inc. in any way.

Library of Congress Control Number: 2004092652
ISBN: 0-9728398-1-X

FIRST EDITION
Printed in the United States of America

To Hyperion and Mochi

We are indebted to many people for help with research, including Imagineers John Hench, Tony Baxter, Bruce Gordon, Joe Lanzisero, Kim Irvine, Doug Hartwell, Bob Baranick, Eddie Sotto, Bob Gurr, Chris Merritt, Josh Shipley, Scott L Jordan, Russell Brower, Bill Watkins, and countless other Imagineers who contributed their knowledge and expertise.

Great credit must also go to our friends and Cast Members Bob Penfield, Roberta Brubaker, Jacob Kahla, and Marty Klein, who along with many others provided contributions both large and small.

We would like to extend our gratitude to Margaret Adamic at Disney Editions and David R. Smith and his knowledgeable crew at the Walt Disney Archives for their assistance in helping us adhere to Walt Disney Company guidelines and trademarks.

Preface

Kevin Yee and Jason Schultz have put together a delightful collection of facts about one of my favorite places in the world, namely Disneyland. I was present at Disneyland's opening in 1955 -- and here's another little known fact: that was the day I presented my fiancé, Patty Dailey, with her engagement ring, while riding on the Mark Twain -- and I wouldn't even try to count the times I've been back since. And I must tell you, there are a lot of things in this book that I didn't know either!

So sit back, relax, let your mind pass through the turnstiles, travel under the railroad station, and look for a whole collection of things you probably wouldn't have known about without this book.

Roy E. Disney

Foreword

Been on INDIANA JONES over a hundred times? Know TOM SAWYER ISLAND like your own backyard? Here is a fun book to read that will take you through Disneyland on a unique journey of discovery. "101 THINGS" will give you plenty of reasons to go back to the Park and experience it all again.

Disneyland is an amazing collection of details. In fact, from a financial standpoint it's practically impossible to justify the importance of the individual ingredients that make the Park special. As someone who had a major role in continuing the enchantment of Disneyland, it is wonderful to see a major work devoted to the details that we at Walt Disney Imagineering refer to as the "Disney Difference." So sit back and get set to enjoy a special journey into the little things that make the Magic Kingdom of Disneyland magical!

Tony Baxter

Main Street, U.S.A.

1

The two roads that bisect Main Street have names: Plaza Street and Center Street.

Both cross streets are clearly visible in the layout of the sidewalk curbs. Though unmarked by signs now, there had originally been street signs listing the street names. Center Street, halfway up Main Street, is formed by the two side alleys, one of which leads to the locker facility. Plaza Street is less obvious. Crossing Main Street at Refreshment Corner, Plaza Street is home to the Main Street Photo Supply, First Aid, and the Baby Center.

FURTHERMORE: Edison Square and Liberty Street are two of the past proposed additions to Main Street. Liberty Street would have featured "One Nation Under God," which included a Hall of Presidents and a Hall of the Declaration of Independence, while the Edison Square project focused on the advent of electricity and its uses. The designs for the various sets of Edison Square were used almost intact for Progressland at the 1964 World's Fair. The Carousel of Progress show was the part of Progressland brought back to Disneyland and housed in the building later used for America Sings and Innoventions.

2

The first four locomotives on the Disneyland Railroad were named after executives from the Santa Fe railroad company.

C.K. Holliday was the founder of the company, E.P. Ripley its first president, Fred Gurley was chairman of the company in 1955, and Ernest S. Marsh was president of the company in 1955. Originally, the Disneyland Railroad was called the Santa Fe & Disneyland Railroad, because the Santa Fe company helped sponsor it.

FURTHERMORE: The first two engines, C.K. Holliday and E.P. Ripley, were built for Disneyland, but the next two added (Fred Gurley and Ernest S. Marsh) had been working locomotives. The Gurley was built in 1895 and had been found on a Louisiana sugar plantation, while the Marsh was built in 1925 and had worked in a New Jersey rock quarry. Walt had a special attraction to Santa Fe, which operated the locomotives that ran through his boyhood home of Marceline, Missouri.

3

Walt's wife Lillian was the inspiration for the name of the V.I.P. parlor car on the Disneyland Railroad.

The coach was transformed in 1974 — just in time for the nation's Bicentennial celebration — from the caboose-like observation car "Grand Canyon" into the opulent parlor car "Lilly Belle." The first Guests of the lush parlor car were Japanese Emperor Hirohito and his wife, visiting the U.S. for the Bicentennial.

FURTHERMORE: The Lilly Belle is also the name of the small-scale locomotive Walt personally built for the miniature railroad in the backyard of his Holmby Hills home, using materials and expertise from the studio's machine shop. The Lilly Belle miniature locomotive or replicas of it are often on display in the Main Street, U.S.A. Train Station.

4

Disneyland projects faux swamp fumes in the Disneyland Railroad's Primeval World to complete a sense of atmospheric immersion.

The fake smells in the diorama give the illusion of actually "being there," and inspired a similar trick at the Universe of Energy pavilion at Epcot. The Candy Palace and the Gibson Girl Ice Cream Parlor on Main Street emit the odor of fresh candy into the street via "smellitzers" (a play of words on the large "howitzer" guns of the World War II era). This trick is also reproduced at Disney's California Adventure, where travelers on Soarin' Over California experience the scents of pine trees, ocean salt, and orange groves.

FURTHERMORE: The distinctive music played during the Primeval World diorama, written by Bernard Hermann, is the prelude music to the movie *Mysterious Island*, the 1961 film based on Verne's sequel to the book *20,000 Leagues Under the Sea*. The sequel takes place on an island populated by enormous exotic beasts. The more sedate melody in the Grand Canyon Diorama is titled "On the Trail," from the Grand Canyon Suite, written by Ferde Grofé.

5

The gas lamps along Main Street are authentic antique street lamps from Baltimore and Philadelphia.

Most of these lamps are 150 years old, purchased for three cents a pound from the cities that had no further use for them. On December 22, 1982, the lamps proved their usefulness when the Park had to be evacuated due to a power outage — the first time that an evacuation of the entire Park was necessary.

FURTHERMORE: The cannons in Town Square are authentic French cannons once owned by the French Army in the nineteenth century. However, they were never fired in battle. Their barrels have been filled in, so they are no longer functional.

6

Many of the windows along the second story of Main Street are decorated with the names of important individuals that made significant contributions to Disneyland.

From Van Arsdale France, the founder of the Disney University, to Bob Penfield, the last original "Cast Member" to retire from Disneyland, the windows pay tribute to those who designed, built, and operated Disneyland over the years. Additional windows honor those who were important in Walt Disney's life.

FURTHERMORE: Most of the tributes pay whimsical respect to the person's contributions, but there are often inside jokes as well. Artist and designer Ken Anderson, for example, was an avid fly fisher, yet his window mentions a fictional bait company – the joke being that fly fishing uses no bait.

7

Disneyland's City Hall is designed after a county court house in Fort Collins, Colorado.

Main Street U.S.A.'s chief designer Harper Goff had grown up in Fort Collins, but didn't tell Walt about his inspiration because he feared Walt would disapprove. In fact, much of Main Street's architectural style is based on the Colorado city, though certain features were lifted wholesale from pictures of Victorian buildings found in art books. The initial idea for Main Street, of course, was to replicate Walt's boyhood home of Marceline, Missouri, but few designs were copied directly from Marceline structures.

FURTHERMORE: Walt asked this same designer to create a saloon for the Golden Horseshoe Revue. Walt told him to mimic the saloon in the 1953 musical *Calamity Jane*, but what Walt didn't know was that Goff had also created the set for that movie in the first place. Originally, the Disneyland saloon was supposed to be themed to Paul Bunyan, then Pecos Bill, but it eventually became Slue Foot Sue's when Pepsi-Cola was brought on board as sponsor. Glass etchings of Pecos Bill and Slue Foot Sue still grace the interior of the establishment near the entrance.

8

The eucalyptus trees behind City Hall were instrumental in the layout of Disneyland.

In the original plans for Disneyland, True-Life Adventureland was situated next to Tomorrowland on the park's east side. The grove of tall, mature eucalyptus trees already growing on the site, however, provided such a good backdrop for Adventureland that the plans were changed to place the land on the park's west side.

FURTHERMORE: The change of location wasn't the only alteration in store for the original five lands. Along with "Frontier Country" and the "World of Tomorrow," True-Life Adventureland would undergo a name change at Imagineer Herb Ryman's suggestion to achieve symmetry as "lands," and they were renamed to the familiar Frontierland, Tomorrowland, and Adventureland.

9

A lamp burns in Walt's honor above the Fire Department, in what had been his private apartment.

Furnished in a rich Victorian style and maintained even today, this apartment enabled Walt to work late and start quickly the next day during Disneyland's construction and early years. By tradition, the lamp in the window was turned on when Walt was on property, to let everyone know he was around.

FURTHERMORE: The Disney Gallery in New Orleans Square was designed to be a new apartment for Walt. Dorothea Redmond designed the 3,000 square foot living space as a larger living quarters for Walt and his guests, but he died before he could move in. The location was ideal because it provided easy upstairs access to the V.I.P. restaurant Club 33 right next door.

10

"Great Moments with Mr. Lincoln" got its start at the 1964 World's Fair.

Several current Disneyland attractions can also trace their origins here. This fair provided five new attractions for Disneyland initially. The State of Illinois sponsored "Great Moments with Mr. Lincoln," while General Electric sponsored Progressland, which later transferred to Disneyland as the Carousel of Progress. Pepsi-Cola and UNICEF sponsored "it's a small world," while the Disneyland Railroad's Primeval World diorama came from the Ford Rotunda presentation, and the Rotunda's "Magic Skyway" vehicle system was adapted at Disneyland in the form of the PeopleMover.

FURTHERMORE: The *Audio-Animatronics* of early mankind in the time-travelling Rotunda show were deemed too crude for Disneyland and were consigned to the junkyard instead. The climactic dinosaur fight from the Rotunda, an homage to a similar scene in *Fantasia*, was originally designed with an allosaurus instead of a tyrannosaurus rex because its opponent – the stegosaurus – was not a contemporary of the T-rex. Disney had received criticism of the scene in *Fantasia* featuring the T-rex and the stegosaurus, so the idea was to aim for historical accuracy in the World's Fair presentation while still paying homage to the film. Nevertheless, the final version featured the familiar T-rex anyway.

11

The Indian statue along Main Street has an identical twin in Frontierland.

Both Indians once served thematic purposes that paid homage to historical trends as well as stereotypes: the Indian on Main Street stood before a tobacconist shop (now 20th Century Music Company) while the one in Frontierland was located in front of a general store.

FURTHERMORE: Both statues are now somewhat out of place. With the tobacco theme gone on Main Street, this Indian serves no thematic purpose. The Frontierland Indian has fared little better; the original themes of Frontierland (there were seven, including one set in 1860) relied heavily on a Native American presence, but now is focused more on Mark Twain's Mississippi delta and the deserts of the Southwest. Meanwhile, the onetime general store has become a candy store.

12

Some elements of the Plaza Inn come from a mansion Walt bought and dismantled.

Walt Disney himself aided in the design of this Victorian-era themed restaurant and he contributed some of the décor from a Victorian mansion he'd recently bought, the St. James mansion, which had been built in 1870, near Adams and Figueroa in Los Angeles. Contributed items included the cut-glass front door and some of the trim along the Palm Room. The 1999 refurbishment of the restaurant preserved many of the features Walt had designed.

FURTHERMORE: The Plaza Inn isn't the only restaurant in Disneyland to preserve history. The soda fountain counter from the movie *The Happiest Millionaire* was incorporated into the serving line at Café Orleans, while an elegant phone booth from the same movie found a home in Club 33. Elsewhere in Club 33, an unassuming table from *Mary Poppins* now graces the main hallway.

13

The infant in a prominent picture at the Baby Care Center is none other than Walt himself.

Walt's image is also prominently visible in pictures at The Walt Disney Story. In fact, one such picture added to celebrate the 100th Anniversary of Walt's birthday is the same infant picture seen in the Baby Care Center. Walt's most visible presence comes from the "Partners" statue at the Central Plaza.

FURTHERMORE: In the "Partners" statue in the Central Plaza of Disneyland, Walt is wearing a tie tack fashioned of three letters: STR, which stood for "Smoke Tree Ranch," his personal retreat and a working ranch. He wore this same tie tack often during televised appearances, including one such video of Walt that was shown in the queue for the Rocket Rods. This statue also shows Walt in his favorite shirt, with a ring containing a bit of the Blarney Stone.

14

A prominent bandstand from Disneyland's early days now lives on at Roger's Gardens in Newport Beach.

At first, the bandstand was positioned at the center of Town Square on Main Street, where the flag pole now stands. However, this placement interfered with the sightline of Sleeping Beauty Castle, and the bandstand was therefore moved next to the Castle even before the Park's Grand Opening.

FURTHERMORE: The subsequent construction of a permanent performance location at Plaza Gardens left no room for a bandstand. It was then moved to Frontierland, to a secluded area known as Magnolia Park, near the present-day location of the Blue Bayou. In 1962, with the Jungle Cruise expanding near the area, the bandstand had seen its final days at the Park.

Adventureland

15

The "huts" atop the Tiki Room roof contain speakers added during the 1996 adjustment to the attraction.

When the Offenbach Barcarolle was removed from the show to shorten the presentation, designers discovered that the sound system had greatly degraded over the years. After returning to the original recordings and cleaning them, they hired a professional concert company to come to the Tiki Room and position speakers to optimize sound. Their placement determined where in the ceiling new cabinets would be created to house the speakers. Subwoofers were also added under the seats.

FURTHERMORE: Many of the tiki carvings at the entrance to Adventureland are originals, dating back to the opening of Disneyland. Hand-carved by Imagineer Harper Goff (whose credits also include set design on *Willy Wonka and the Chocolate Factory*) in his garage, the carvings have endured the decades of weathering without much aging, and even withstood transplantation during the widening of the Adventureland bridge in 1994. This contribution, as well as his work as art director for the Jungle Cruise, led Goff to the distinction of having a window bear his name at Disneyland, but not on Main Street like everyone else – his is above the shops in Adventureland.

16

The smaller mechanical birds used in the Tiki Room were originally conceived as an addition to the Rainbow Caverns Mine Train.

Walt's obsession with mechanical birds reached a fever pitch when designers began work on a robotic Confucius (which would later develop into the Lincoln project), and the plan at the time was to create an expansion of the Rainbow Caverns attraction specifically to make use of the birds.

FURTHERMORE: Later, the bird show would evolve into its own show. The first idea was to transform the planned Confucius restaurant into a singing bird restaurant, and the modern-day presence of bathrooms at the Tiki Room pay testament to this plan to house a restaurant. As the show came together, the Tiki Room was almost sent to the pivotal 1964 World's Fair as a fifth Disney exhibit, to be sponsored by Coca-Cola, but the plans fell through at the last moment.

17

One of the macaws off to the side in the Tiki Room was once the barker bird which sat perched outside the Tiki Room to generate interest in the attraction.

This specific mechanical avian was one of two to serve as the barker bird, who was so popular that it created bottlenecks on the narrow bridge. It was retired to an office, but was resurrected seventeen years later, dusted off, given new feathers, and put back in the show as one of the "side" macaws.

FURTHERMORE: A small brass birdcage with a mechanical bird from New Orleans, Louisiana served as the inspiration for the Enchanted Tiki Room's animated birds and the process of *Audio-Animatronics* so pivotal to Disney's theme park storytelling. This birdcage sat in Walt's formal office when the offices were moved after Walt's death to Disneyland, where it remained for many years. When Walt's "working" office was relocated to Walt Disney World for the "100 Years of Magic" celebration in 2001, the birdcage was transferred to the "working" office and made its way to Florida.

18

One palm tree at the Jungle Cruise had grown on the property long before Disney bought the land.

The giant palm tree to the right side of the Jungle Cruise entrance building was owned by the Dominguez family, who owned some of the property Disneyland was built upon. Planted in 1896, the Canary Islands date palm had been a onetime wedding present and was passed down through the generations. When Walt bought the property, he agreed to preserve the palm tree, and it was moved from its original location, which was to become part of the parking lot, over to Adventureland.

FURTHERMORE: Great care was taken in 1994 when rebuilding the Jungle Cruise queue building so as not to destroy the Dominguez Palm. The tree's position made the new queue building a challenge, as they had wanted to expand into this area, so as a compromise the building was constructed right up against the tree with no room to spare.

19

The Jungle Cruise queue building was designed to imply that Nature is overtaking the structure.

The building is intentionally sinking on one side, and gaps in the rooftops and railings testify to invasive tree branches. Displays of dead scorpions in the upstairs queue further the notion that Nature is dangerous, as does a threatening cobra among the rafters.

FURTHERMORE: The building is themed as an abandoned European colonialist venture that evolved into a water safari for tourists. The British flag betrays the initial English presence, while the French words scattered about the signs refer to its role as the international language before World War II. Once the European governments left, the remaining soldiers began a tour business. An infirmary had to be added, since a jungle is inherently dangerous. Today the infirmary serves as a foreshadowing that the jungle may not be perfectly tame.

20

The boats on the Jungle Cruise are themed to look like the boat in the movie *The African Queen.*

The 1951 Humphrey Bogart and Katherine Hepburn film provided some of the inspiration for the look of the Jungle Cruise. The theme was given extra weight in the 1994 rehab, when designers crafted a new queue building and changed the boat designs from a colorful, cartoony canvas to a more realistic, 1930s-style boat with faded and worn canvas. The cartoony boats live on in memories, however, and in the remote-controlled boats at the Disneyland Hotel, added in 1999, which were given the Jungle Cruise's old look of red-and-white striped canvas. Hotel Guests can use the remote-controlled safari boats to move through certain obstacles and trigger events like a boat burning, an elephant spraying water, or a bridge quaking from an angry gorilla.

FURTHERMORE: One gag seldom noticed in the Jungle Cruise is a box containing the initials of the design arm of the company – specifically, the old name of that division, W.E.D. (which stood for Walter Elias Disney). The crate in question is labeled "WED Safari" and can be found in the tent where the gorillas have overturned the jeep and are now ransacking the guns and equipment in the tent.

21

A sign from Disneyland's old parking lot is concealed in the queue for the Indiana Jones Adventure.

Because the attraction was built in a new structure that jutted out into the then-existing parking lot, it took over part of the space formerly named the Eeyore parking lot. Clever Imagineers preserved one of the blue "Eeyore" signs and placed it near the ceiling in the "slideshow room" of the queue, near the projector and mostly hidden by bamboo slats.

FURTHERMORE: The ride designers concealed their own initials with the identifying numbers for each of the Troop Transports, the vehicles Guests use in the attraction. The long tradition of designers hiding their initials can also be seen on license plates at Autopia and on pipes in the Star Tours queue. Cryptic scribblings around Tomorrowland in "Da Vinci script" disguise still more names. Since Leonardo Da Vinci wrote in his notebooks backward, designers in Tomorrowland recorded their own names backward, using a stylized font.

22

The office in the Indiana Jones Adventure queue references the Indiana Jones movies in several ways.

The office is built as if it were a giant crate, and this "crate" is labeled on the side with "990 6753" – the same numbers that identify the crate containing the Ark of the Covenant in the movie. Also, this "crate" is stamped with the words "Deliver to Club Obi Wan," a reference to a club from the movie series, as well as Lucas' other popular franchise, Star Wars.

FURTHERMORE: The jeep in the outside queue is also a prop: this was the actual vehicle from the pivotal chase scene in the first movie, where Indiana Jones is dragged along the ground at high speed. It's not the only authentic jeep in Adventureland, however. The jeep which houses a fruit cart at the exit to the Tiki Room is a relic from World War II.

23

One branch on Tarzan's Treehouse is from the Swiss Family Treehouse, the attraction's former theme.

One branch and its synthetic leaves were not removed when the rest of the tree was stripped and re-created. It can be found under the final room in the attraction, although it is only visible from below. The phrase "Mind Thy Head," which had been painted on a branch to warn of low clearance, is recreated as a second homage in the revamped tree, but in a different location. As a final tribute, the "Swisskapolka" music that used to play at an organ in the tree can now be heard from a gramophone at the base of the tree. Nearby is a tea set inspired by Mrs. Potts and Chip from *Beauty and the Beast.*

FURTHERMORE: The figures of characters in Tarzan's Treehouse are giant maquettes. Maquettes are small character models useful when creating animated movies. Such small maquettes from the Tarzan movie were digitally scanned in 3-D and then re-created in large scale using a lathe and foamcore. Thus, the poses on the figures were predetermined and sets had to be designed to fit the characters rather than vice-versa. On installation, designers saw that Tarzan's face wasn't very visible, and the idea to use a mirror was born, so that Guests would be able to see Tarzan's face if they turned around when leaving that room.

New Orleans
Square

24

The sails visible along the roofline of New Orleans Square were installed to cover giant searchlights.

In 1994, Disneyland began "The Lights Fantastic," a network of gigantic searchlights positioned at various points around the Park, where the colored beams could synchronize in a nighttime display. Each searchlight was 7,000 watts and fully automated, with twenty-one total in the park: five atop Pirates of the Caribbean, five at Mission to Mars, five more behind Toontown, and three on each side of Fantasyland. An Herb Ryman conceptual painting of New Orleans Square, created to provide tone before more specific designs were drawn, includes just such a scene of sails peeking over the roofline, and this view inspired designers to capture Ryman's original concept when covering up the Lights Fantastic.

FURTHERMORE: Spotlights are part of New Orleans Square's past in another respect as well. When Pirates of the Caribbean was first conceived as a walk-through attraction, most of story would have unfolded on one large set. Various parts of the set would be lit by spotlights as a sole *Audio-Animatronics* pirate narrated a story. Walt returned from the 1964-1965 World's Fair with an understanding for moving large amounts of Guests, and knew he'd have to abandon the walk-through concept for key attractions like the Pirates one.

25

The frequent groupings of American, French and Spanish flags in New Orleans Square refer to the onetime governments of the Louisiana city.

There have been several governments in New Orleans, including England, Louisiana, and West Florida, but the three with the largest influence are honored in Disneyland by placing small flags together at various points in the land, always on the second story.

FURTHERMORE: The area between Pirates of the Caribbean and Tarzan's Treehouse is a Pirate's Alley that mirrors an actual "Pirate's Alley" in New Orleans. Just like the real Pirate's Alley next to famous Jackson Square, Disneyland's version is characterized by foliage on one side and typical New Orleans architecture on the other.

26

The tiered esplanade in New Orleans Square was inspired by Factor's Walk in Savannah, Georgia.

The granite in the famous seaside Factor's Walk is not native to below-sea-level Georgia, but had been shipped over as ballast in the ships of the English settlers. The ballast was crushed to make walkways, and the ships were filled with cotton for a return voyage. Disney designers wanted to approximate the look of crushed ballast, but had to move gradually from that rough texture along the waterline to the more refined streets of New Orleans, so the esplanade features different textures to make the transition gradual.

FURTHERMORE: The need for an authentic appearance did not prevent designers from substituting materials when it suited them. Designers used black rubber rather than iron for the railings of second-floor balconies throughout the land whenever the balcony was purely decorative and not meant to be visited. They knew that iron would be subject to rust, while rubber stood a better chance of weathering the elements for years.

27

A canal in New Orleans Square, labeled "1764," is all that remains of a plan to unify several themes in the land.

The plan called for a crypt next to the Mansion that led into an underground catacomb of treasure and dead pirates, culminating in a pirate-themed hideout on Tom Sawyer Island. The pirate theme would have focused on Jean Laffite, a real-life pirate from the early 1800s in New Orleans. Laffite's name might be familiar to frequent Disneyland visitors from the Pirates of the Caribbean loading zone, where a sign reads "Laffite's Landing." The date 1764 was derived by subtracting 200 years from the birth date of one Imagineer who worked on the project.

FURTHERMORE: Before its replacement with La Petite Patisserie, there was also a Laffite's Silver Shop in New Orleans Square. Having a Jean Laffite identified as the "owner" of the Haunted Mansion would have united Pirates of the Caribbean with the Mansion and the island into one underlying theme, an unusual feat for an entire land. Though unrealized, the plan lives on in the form of this barricaded "crypt."

28

"Fantasmic!" was originally named "Imagination."

The original title made sense, because the show would focus on Mickey Mouse's rampant imagination as it was overrun by the forces of evil. Remnants of this theme can be heard throughout the show's soundtrack: references to imagination punctuate the dialogue as well as the musical theme.

FURTHERMORE: Promotional artwork was first drawn up with an "Imagination" logo. Before its premiere the name changed, but not yet to "Fantasmic!" Instead, the show was dubbed "Phantasmagoria." That latter word had been copyrighted over 30 times in the United States, however, so designers again changed the name and came up with the now-familiar "Fantasmic!"

29

Walt's and Roy's initials can be seen on a balcony at the Disney Gallery.

Ornate versions of "WD" and "RD" look out over the balcony of Walt's intended apartment, an idea that comes from the city of New Orleans. Baroness Micaela Almonester de Pontalba built apartments near famous Jackson Square that were the very first to feature decorative cast iron railings – the feature which would become the city's hallmark. Her "AP" initials can still be seen among the railings in the Louisiana city.

FURTHERMORE: The distinctive spire atop Pirates of the Caribbean imitates another New Orleans landmark: the Cabildo in Jackson Square. Built in 1799 to house the Spanish colonial government, the Cabildo became famous in 1803 when the purchase of the Louisiana Territory was signed here.

30

Some *Audio-Animatronics* figures in Pirates of the Caribbean come from Epcot.

The 1997 refurbishment of Pirates of the Caribbean saw the addition of several robotic performers that were removed from World of Motion at Epcot, when that attraction closed to make room for Test Track. Characters, including a horse, were added to the chase scenes. Other figures were installed at the end of the ride, where two greedy pirates struggle to move an overflowing treasure chest. Less immediately visible are conquistador-style soldiers peering over the battlements of the fort in the battle scene.

FURTHERMORE: The skeletons in the ride were originally real specimens, but have since been replaced by artificial facsimiles. Reproductions of skeletons were not convincing in the 1960s, so actual ones were obtained from the University of California Medical Center where they had been used for research. Later, when they were replaced by lifelike models, they were returned to their originating country and given a proper burial.

31

The pirate ship attacking the fort is named the "Wicked Wench."

The ship's name is scrawled across the stern of the ship, and thus is not visible to Guests floating past. There are other "wenches" in the ride, such as the infamous "wench" auction, or "wench-chasing" *Audio-Animatronics* turntables that were altered in the 1990s to show pirates chasing food. Even the Guest boats themselves are "wenches," since they had female names until the original boats were replaced, then regained female names in 2003's refurbishment. The prevalence of faux femininity has a cumulative tongue-in-cheek effect, and feminizes both performers and audience: we are all "wenches" in the attraction, with the pirates playing the role of Wicked Wenches.

FURTHERMORE: The pirate captain was one of the first of a new generation of *Audio-Animatronics*. Called "sarcos" figures after the company which designed it (in turn named after the Greek word for "muscle"), these figures are so realistic primarily because of a new feature called compliance: they are able to anticipate the end of a stroke of movement and thus cushion its stop. Older *Audio-Animatronics* figures could vary the speed of their movements, but without the ability to anticipate the end of the stroke, the figures invariably twanged and wiggled unnaturally when motion stopped.

32

The fortune teller in Pieces of Eight is a remnant of the former "Pirates Arcade" in this same space.

When Pirates of the Caribbean opened in 1967, the location next to its exit was not yet a shop as it is today. This facility, more an arcade than anything else, featured such coin-operated contraptions as the fortune teller "Old Red," who dispensed cards of advice, as well as a machine which personalized "pieces of eight," or Spanish doubloons. Visitors could even buy Pirates concept art in the form of postcards from a nearby vending machine.

FURTHERMORE: There were also shooting gallery machines here, of the electro-magnetic variety also seen for many years in Adventureland. The Pirates Arcade Museum included "Freebooter Shooter," "Cap'n Black," and "Captain Hook," which played music from the movie *Peter Pan*.

33

There is an unpublicized members-only club on the second story of New Orleans Square.

Club 33, as it's known, was intended to be a place for Walt to host visiting dignitaries and executives from sponsoring companies. The 33 original sponsors of Disneyland reportedly gives the club its name, though this claim is often disputed. The Red Wagon Inn (now Plaza Inn) hosted a modest private club since the park's earliest days, but the idea for a bigger parkwide club was revitalized during Disney's heavy involvement in the 1964 World's Fair, where numerous companies offered private lounges to VIPs at their pavilions.

FURTHERMORE: Walt died before Club 33 opened, and membership is now open to the public, though it requires annual fees and has a long waiting list. The Club is located on 33 Royal Street, and while non-members may not normally visit inside, they can easily locate the restaurant's entry door. Next to the Blue Bayou is an unremarkable door decorated on the side with a glittering "33" mirrored sign.

34

Talking heads along the walls of Club 33 were supposed to be animated, to provide an interactive experience while dining.

Performing *Audio-Animatronics* figures in the "Trophy Room" – complete with animated animal heads – would keep Guests entertained while they ate. Walt died before plans could be finished. Today, the room has been renamed the "Disney Room," and all that remains of the animals is a vulture that lurks in one corner, wired but never activated.

FURTHERMORE: A different kind of proposed interactivity involved microphones implanted in the chandelier overhead; the kitchen staff could overhear if diners needed anything, and then respond without ever having been asked directly. Deemed an invasion of privacy before it could be used as intended, the microphone remains in the chandelier but has never been activated.

35

The weathervane atop the Haunted Mansion is one of the remnants of the attraction's backstory.

The antebellum house is ostensibly owned by a wealthy sailor named Captain Gore, circa 1810, who desires to take a bride named Priscilla. She agrees, but soon after realizes he is in fact a pirate. He kills her in a rage, but she haunts him, eventually leading him to commit suicide as he cannot escape her. The weathervane — a ship — is one of the few signs that remains of the captain and his story, together with the bride and some nautical paraphernalia in the attic and the hanging body in the gallery. This story, one of three possible backstories written for the attraction, was never fully implemented into the attraction, possibly because Walt's death occurred as the ride's elements began to take form.

FURTHERMORE: The second backstory labeled the Mansion Bloodmere Manor, an ostensible old Southern house transplanted to Disneyland but haunted so thoroughly that no workers could renovate it. The third potential backstory revolved around the Headless Horseman from *The Legend of Sleepy Hollow*. Although this theme was not used, special effects developed for this theme were used in the final attraction, such as lightning flashes and ghosts rising from tombs.

36

A raven is present whenever the "Ghost Host" narrator speaks in the Haunted Mansion.

Each time Guests hear the voice of the Ghost Host, the raven is nearby. Originally, the bird was supposed to *be* the Ghost Host, the narrator of the ride. The raven, long associated with death, is present at the top of the first staircase, in the conservatory on the moving coffin, in the séance room on the chair, in the Ballroom along the rear wall, and at the end of the graveyard, just as visitors enter the crypt. One additional appearance by the raven – as we descend through the trees to the graveyard – is distinguished by the fact that the narrator does not speak at this moment.

FURTHERMORE: One of the Mansion's creepiest optical effects, the busts that appear to turn their heads in sync with any patron that passes by them, actually owes its existence to Great Moments with Mr. Lincoln. Designers happened to pass by a negative mold of the Lincoln head – an inverted cast from which the actual head would be made – when they realized that its inverted nature always resulted in the unnerving effect.

37

The "Tarot Madam" in the Haunted Mansion Holiday is the daughter of the original attraction's "Séance Madam."

Imagineer Kim Irvine, who lends her voice and likeness to the tarot card reader, is the biological daughter of Imagineer Leota Thomas (born Leota Toombs), who provided the face for the Madam Leota character in the original attraction. But Leota was not the voice – that honor went to Eleanor Audley, who also gave voice to Malificent in the film *Sleeping Beauty*. The Séance Madam was recognizable enough to be satirized in Superstar Limo, an ironic postmodern dark ride in Disney's California Adventure.

FURTHERMORE: The miniature ghost at the conclusion of the Haunted Mansion, known as "Little Leota," is also Leota Thomas (in this case, both face and voice). She had originally done the video work for both characters as an in-house dry run, so that designers could have a working model. But they liked her performance so much, no professional actress had to be brought in.

38

The face of a long-gone "Hatbox Ghost" in the Haunted Mansion still exists in the attraction.

Only present for testing and the first few months of operation in 1969, the famed Hatbox Ghost was a character in the attic whose head disappeared, only to reappear in the hatbox he held to one side. This character's face can still be seen in a portrait just above the "Tomb Sweet Tomb" sign in the hallway before the séance room. Even more prominently, his is also the face of the tall hitchhiker at the end of the ride.

FURTHERMORE: The Hatbox Ghost's face is not the only familiar visage to the sharp-eyed Disneyland visitor. One of the duelists in the ghostly portraits of the Grand Hall is none other than the auctioneer from Pirates of the Caribbean. Even the round-faced Hitchhiking Ghost, unofficially dubbed Ezra, is used a few times throughout the attraction.

39

The organ in the Haunted Mansion ballroom is a prop from the *20,000 Leagues Under the Sea* movie and subsequent Disneyland exhibit.

The Tomorrowland exhibit closed just before the Haunted Mansion opened, offering designers an ideal chance to re-use some of the props. The organ formerly played Bach's "Toccata and Fugue in D minor" in the exhibit, and it needed but scant redecorating before its installation in the Haunted Mansion.

FURTHERMORE: The ballroom scene utilizes an old magician's technique called "Pepper's Ghost": actual robots and mannequins are going through the motions that patrons witness, but these mannequins are located directly above and directly below the level the Guests are on. Lighting thrown on them gets reflected in the plate glass between visitors and the ballroom, making it seem that the images inhabit the empty set below. Because the reflection shows a mirror image, sharp-eyed visitors will notice that the women are leading the men in the dance. This same technique is also used in Pinocchio's Daring Journey to make the Blue Fairy disappear.

40

One statue in the Haunted Mansion attic has a twin on Main Street.

The attic's unobtrusive white statue of a girl holding a pot on one shoulder has a twin in an equally hidden location: in the former Guided Tours Garden, the small patio adjacent to City Hall where guided tours would begin. This commonly seen cement statue depicts the Biblical Rebecca carrying water from the well.

FURTHERMORE: Some portions of the Haunted Mansion are thematic remnants of the original proposed idea to house a "museum of the weird" in the building, which was to be the first part of the attraction when conceived as a walk-through. The designs featured monstrous meldings of body parts and furniture, and these ideas live on today: the armchair near the "endless hallway" forms a giant face; the hallway clock striking thirteen is being swallowed by a monster with sharp teeth (the clock's twisted pendulum is actually his tail); and the candelabras at the end of the attraction are held up by disembodied arms, to name only a few examples.

Critter Country

41

The man most responsible for constructing Disneyland is honored in several ways in Critter Country.

Retired Admiral Joe Fowler's name can be seen in two places: the drydock for the big boats is called Fowler's Harbor (giving rise, in turn, to Harbour Galley's name), and a nearby door after the big drop on Splash Mountain is labeled as Fowler's Cellar.

FURTHERMORE: Mill View Lane, emblazoned on a sign right next to Harbour Galley's service windows, is also a Fowler reference: he lived on Mill View Lane when he worked in Florida, helping with the construction of Walt Disney World. A sign on the nearby shack used to advertise "Maurie's Lobster Dinners." While lobsters were not sold anywhere, they were yet another nod to Fowler, whose wife was named Maurie. In a 1956 billboard announcing Tom Sawyer Island, the building now called Harbour Galley was listed as the Magnetic House, as part of a never-built addition named "River Town," to be situated near Magnolia Park and to feature novelty shops.

42

The canoes attractions used to be themed to Indians, not Davy Crockett.

The first canoes were smaller, shorter, and narrower than today's version, and they sat only one rider per row. Launched from Frontierland, the canoes were a continuation of the Indian Village, where actual Indians lived and performed daily shows. The Briar Patch shop, another remnant from that era, was originally named the Indian Trading Post. Somewhat incongruously, Disneyland's Indians had never used a canoe before they moved into the park.

FURTHERMORE: The Indian Village was located near present-day Critter Country, though back then not even Bear Country had been opened. After one relocation, the village took on new life in the backwaters of the Rivers of America, this time with *Audio-Animatronics* figures rather than living Native Americans.

43

Stuffed heads of Max, Melvin, and Buff in the final scene of the Many Adventures of Winnie the Pooh pay tribute to the Country Bear Playhouse that preceded it.

These three heads could be found long ago in the Mile Long Bar (later Brer Bar) and were not animated robots, but simple models. When the Country Bears moved out, the stuffed heads were added to the Many Adventures of Winnie the Pooh as a way of nodding to the history of this location.

FURTHERMORE: A version of Melvin the Moose, from the Country Bear Playhouse, can also be seen in Mr. Toad's Wild Ride: a two-dimensional painting of the simple-minded moose, often teased by the other "talking heads" of the Country Bear shows, appears in Winky's Pub in the middle of the attraction.

44

Many of the "critters" in Splash Mountain come from America Sings, a former attraction in Tomorrowland.

Most of the animated characters in Splash Mountain do not appear in *Song of the South*, the movie which provides the theme for the ride, and come directly from an *Audio-Animatronics* musical show in Tomorrowland. Their presence, which is especially strong at the finale, helps round out the fictional Splash Mountain world but does not always fit the theme perfectly. The "Laughin' Place," for instance, features numerous gopher holes – out of which pops a weasel rather than a gopher.

FURTHERMORE: Although the literal themes of the two attractions might seem to clash, there are definite stylistic similarities. Animator Marc Davis drew many of the conceptual drawings for the critters in *Song of the South*, and he later used a similar style when designing figures for America Sings. Both attractions are united by a common artistic vision, and the critters which eventually found their way into Splash Mountain therefore automatically fit the style and characterization of the *Song of the South*.

45

The snoring sound effect in a cave on Splash Mountain formerly belonged to Rufus the Country Bear.

Before Splash Mountain existed, Guests entering Bear Country were greeted by the sound of Rufus snoring in a cave on a hill. When Splash Mountain opened, the sound effect was continued at a cave before Slippin' Falls, the first drop. After a short time, however, designers realized that Rufus didn't really fit the theme of Splash Mountain, and the sign outside the cave was changed to Br'er Bear's name.

FURTHERMORE: This snoring sound effect has an interesting history all its own; in fact, it's the oldest sound effect in use at Disneyland. It was originally recorded in the 1930s for *Snow White and the Seven Dwarfs*, but was never used in the film. It first found a home at the hotel in Frontierland's Rainbow Ridge, then was moved to the Bear Country Cave and finally relocated to the lair in Splash Mountain.

46

There is a whimsical sign at the base of the drop on Splash Mountain.

Riders whizzing by at 40 mph may not always notice it, but there is a signpost to the right side of the logs as they splash down from the drop. The sign reads: "Drop in Again Sometime." Disneyland took great pride in the fact that Splash Mountain featured the world's tallest and steepest drop for a flume ride when it opened.

FURTHERMORE: Imagineer Tony Baxter conceived of Splash Mountain while sitting in traffic on the freeway. He realized the need for a big attraction in this corner of the Park and knew the *Audio-Animatronics* from the under-attended America Sings attraction in Tomorrowland could be made available, and he hit upon the large animal cast of *Song of the South* as an ideal theme to unite the available robots with the need for a big attraction.

Frontierland

47

The original Frontierland Railroad Station now sits on the opposite side of the train tracks.

Guests stood in line for the train by passing through the depot, a full-size structure. This train station had been reconstructed from blueprints for a station set built for the 1949 feature *So Dear to My Heart*. The original movie prop had been given to Ward Kimball, a Disney Studio employee and fellow railroad enthusiast, and he didn't want to give it back.

FURTHERMORE: The expansion of New Orleans Square necessitated moving the structure to the other side of the tracks, where it remains today as a storeroom, with props still glued to the walls from its days as a viewable onstage piece of Disneyland. This structure was used as a backdrop for a scene in the old slideshow at "Great Moments with Mr. Lincoln," and was the inspiration for the Toontown Train Station, which was built to be a cartoon version of the same shape. The Frontierland Railroad Station isn't the only one to have seen double duty; today's Tomorrowland Railroad Station was once the station for the Viewliner train.

48

The telegraph at the Frontierland Train Station types out part of Walt's Opening Day speech.

The landline telegraphy used by railroaders slowly taps out the words: "To all who come to this happy place, welcome," which was the first sentence of Walt's dedication of Disneyland.

FURTHERMORE: In the very early days, the station tapped out ribald messages, but these were quickly changed to the dedication speech when Walt remarked off-handedly that his wife Lillian had been trained as a telegraph operator and could decipher landline telegraphy. The recording degraded over the years, but it wasn't until the 1990s that a visitor with the proper training recognized the broken sequence and informed park officials, who promptly had the recording changed.

49

Tom Sawyer Island was originally supposed to be named Mickey Mouse Island.

During the planning stages of Disneyland, Walt wanted to house the Mouseketeers and the Mickey Mouse Club on the island, but later switched to the themes and characters from Mark Twain to better fit Frontierland's rugged Western theme.

FURTHERMORE: The Mouseketeers were introduced to television on Disneyland's opening day – the *Mickey Mouse Club* show did not air until later. The Mickey Mouse Club Theater in Fantasyland was related to the Club only in name; it wasn't until 1963 that the Mouseketeers had a headquarters at Disneyland, displacing the *Babes in Toyland* exhibit in the Opera House.

50

Walt Disney designed the shoreline of Tom Sawyer Island himself.

Designers originally attempted a layout, but Walt, dissatisfied, took their plans home with him and returned with a completely revamped design that emphasized discovery and exploration via bridges, footpaths, and caves. Several points on the island are named after people in Walt's life; one such example, Sharon Inlet, was named after his daughter.

FURTHERMORE: Over the years, the island has had many changes. The major subterranean cave, known as "Injun' Joe's," reversed direction to ease crowd flow on the island. Fort Wilderness once featured a secret escape in the event Indians overran the stronghold, but officials have since closed the hidden escape route. The outside end of the secret escape route remains visibly boarded up today.

51

Walt created Tom Sawyer Island as a recreation of a sand spit he'd known as a child in Marceline.

During construction of the fort, Walt instinctively sensed the initial placement wasn't right and asked for a wall to be moved by twenty feet. His brother Roy later explained they had swum out to a sand spit in Marceline and built a fort on several occasions, always to Walt's specifications, so that Tom Sawyer Island became a full-sized version of his childhood fort. He was recreating the Marceline sand spit with his theme park island.

FURTHERMORE: Fort Wilderness was constructed after the island had already been completed and the Rivers of America had been filled in. Logs were brought to the site by truck, and then were floated across the river and lifted out to the island. Just like the stockade at the entrance to Frontierland, Fort Wilderness is constructed out of real logs.

52

The treehouse on Tom Sawyer Island is the "source" for the Rivers of America.

Tom and Huck's Treehouse features an exaggerated root system, out of which flows forceful streams into the Rivers of America. According to legend (and a 1957 map of the island), these streams are the "headwaters" of the Rivers of America – the place where all the water supposedly comes from.

FURTHERMORE: Tom and Huck's Treehouse was also the highest Guest-accessible location when it opened in 1956, since none of the current mountain range yet existed and Sleeping Beauty Castle didn't open its walk-through attraction until 1957.

53

The oldest object in Disneyland is a petrified sequoia redwood tree.

This tree, at least 55 million years old, was purchased by Walt as an anniversary present for Lillian in 1956, who quickly donated it to Disneyland, and installed it along the Rivers of America in September, 1957. The Pike Petrified Forest in Colorado, where Walt had found the tree, featured many such preserved trees. The owner tried to convince Walt to buy the entire petrified forest and bring it to Disneyland.

FURTHERMORE: The oldest cultural artifact ever at Disneyland was a bronze urn by Italian sculptor and goldsmith Benvenuto Cellini. The artifact, which dates back to the 16th century Italian Renaissance, was used in the 20,000 Leagues Under the Sea exhibit in Tomorrowland. The 20,000 Leagues attraction also featured an exhibit case that was displayed in the One-of-a-Kind shop in New Orleans Square for many years.

54

A keelboat named Gullywhumper along the Rivers of America used to be a working attraction.

The original keelboats on the river were props used in the *Davy Crockett* movies, but these were neither large enough nor hardy enough to endure the daily crush of visitors for long, so more durable replicas were built. The Gullywhumper and its sister ship, the Bertha Mae, retired in 1997. The Bertha Mae was sold by online auction to a collector in 2001, but the Gullywhumper was added as a prop to the river in early 2003. The former Keelboat loading dock can still be seen adjacent to the dock for the Tom Sawyer Island rafts.

FURTHERMORE: The Rivers of America was inaugurated with actual water samples from some American waterways. At the dedication of Tom Sawyer Island in 1956, costumed versions of Becky Thatcher and Tom Sawyer introduced a bottle of water from the Mississippi River and also deposited some soil from Jackson's Island in Hannibal, Missouri. The party then moved across the way to the Plantation House to consume 38 pounds of catfish flown in from Missouri. A similar strategy was used at the opening of "it's a small world," which claims that Guests navigate "The Seven Seaways" around the globe. To lend credibility to the claim, Walt inaugurated "it's a small world" by dropping in water samples from each of the world's oceans.

55

A carving of a flying fish in the below-decks museum of the Sailing Ship Columbia has ties to the H.M.S. Bounty.

The carving was created in 1952 by Fred Christian, the grandson of Fletcher Christian – the prime mutineer on the H.M.S. Bounty (made famous by the mutiny against Captain Bligh). The wood for the carving is said to have come from wreckage of the original Bounty. Christian had given the carving to a recreation of the Bounty used for a 1978 movie, and the movie's producers then donated it to the Disneyland attraction in 1985.

FURTHERMORE: Astoundingly, Disneyland's Columbia was built using the plans for the H.M.S. Bounty. When Walt wanted to built a replica of the famous American ship, all that could be found were plans for the H.M.S. Bounty, which was a collier ship similar enough to the Columbia to satisfy Walt.

56

The bell on the Sailing Ship Columbia pays homage to the "real" name of the ship that inspired the attraction.

Engraved on the bell are the words "Columbia Rediviva, Plymouth, Massachusetts, 1787" – which refers to the ship's correct title (Rediviva means "revived") as well as its place and time of creation.

FURTHERMORE: The U.S.S. Columbia was the first American ship to sail around the world, the feat which first endeared Walt to this famous ship. The journey started in 1787 and took three years to complete. The ship discovered the Columbia River; in fact, the river is named after the ship. Disneyland's version was the first windjammer built in America in over 100 years when it was constructed in 1958.

57

Walt's reserved seats at the Golden Horseshoe Saloon can still be seen.

Walt's box on the stage-left side of the theater was kept empty during his lifetime, in case he dropped by for a visit to the show. Keeping seats empty wasn't always easy; the Golden Horseshoe Revue was popular, and it would eventually set a world record for most performances of a live-action show.

FURTHERMORE: The star of the Revue, Wally Boag, also voiced José in the Tiki Room, and at least one joke in the Tiki Room refers back to the Revue. The German-accented bird Fritz at one point says to José, "Isn't that right, Herr Schmidt? Oh, that's right, Schmidt has no hair!" in direct reference to Wally's baldness — a point Wally used to his favor in the Golden Horseshoe show when he removed his wig for a shock laugh.

58

Lettering on a window in Rancho del Zocalo pays homage to Mineral Hall, a shop on this spot in Disneyland's earliest days.

Mineral Hall displayed glowing minerals under "black light," which encouraged Guests to buy some rocks for themselves. The original structure remained during Casa Mexicana's tenure on this spot, and one window pane with the lettering was preserved. The Rancho del Zocalo window is not the original Mineral Hall one – it's larger and located on the second floor – but is nonetheless a tribute to the original tenant of the building.

FURTHERMORE: The original location of Mineral Hall was taken over by Casa de Fritos (later renamed Casa Mexicana), and for years the window pane was left as an afterthought, with the area used as backstage offices. When Rancho del Zocalo premiered, this zone was rebuilt and now visitors to the restaurant walk right through the old Mineral Hall area when they pass through the exit closest to Big Thunder Mountain Railroad.

59

A sign above Rancho del Zocalo pays homage to the restaurant's former name.

A welcoming sign above the entrance reads "mi casa es su casa," which is a reference to the location's most recent name of Casa Mexicana. The first half of Rancho del Zocalo's name honors Big Thunder Ranch, a nearby barbecue restaurant that closed but had its menu folded into the new Rancho del Zocalo.

FURTHERMORE: Rancho del Zocalo takes the latter part of its name from a plaza in Disneyland's earliest days. The circular plaza in the middle of Frontierland was named El Zocalo on early Park maps, and served as the mini-hub in Frontierland from which Guests could board the Pack Mules, Stagecoach, Conestoga Wagons, or Rainbow Caverns Mine Train. This area had a Mexican theme from the beginning: near El Zocalo, close to the Mark Twain dock, was Mexican Imports, a small merchandise location that reinforced the Southwestern flavor of the area.

60

Big Thunder Mountain's name refers to the earthquake in the ride and an ancient curse.

The mountain would supposedly defend itself from any defacement by exacting revenge upon the interlopers. Miners scarred the mountain, and they disappeared from the mine train – that's why tourists ride in an out-of-control train without a crew. The Mark Twain ride narration mentions that Big Thunder is located very close to sacred Indian grounds – thus tying together the roller coaster with the just-seen Indian Village along the Rivers of America.

FURTHERMORE: The even more detailed backstory is that an inventor named Jason Chandler created a revolutionary drilling machine, which he used to rescue miners trapped in the mountain by a cave-in. Chandler discovered an unbelievable vein of gold – enough to render the gold standard useless – so he only slowly cashed in, and used the money to finance Discovery Bay, a sanctuary for scientific development.

61

The town buildings in Big Thunder were recycled from previous attractions on this spot.

Originally, the buildings were more scattered and represented the town of Rainbow Ridge for the Rainbow Caverns Mine Train, and then were later used for Mine Train Through Nature's Wonderland.

FURTHERMORE: The colorful waterfalls at the beginning of Big Thunder Mountain Railroad are a tribute to Rainbow Caverns Mine Train, which culminated in the colorful waterfall displays. The modern cave with colored stalactites and stalagmites may be larger than its predecessor in terms of size, but it does not compare with the original Rainbow Caverns, which had twenty-two such fountains and falls, including Witches' Cauldron, Bridal Veil Falls, Paint Pot Falls, and Red Devil Falls.

62

The steam engine behind Big Thunder Mountain Railroad was a prop in the movie *Hot Lead & Cold Feet* (1978).

The miniature locomotive, situated at the end of Big Thunder Trail, was ostensibly an "iron donkey" workhorse engine in the movie's town of Bloodshy, and used in the lengthy race sequence of the movie. The other locomotive used in the movie also resides at Big Thunder; it sits near the town of Big Thunder and alongside the queue for the attraction. Both are painted to represent engine number 11, the hero's engine in the movie.

FURTHERMORE: Nearly all the set dressings in the Big Thunder Mountain queue area are authentic and placed as they would be in a working mine. The Silver Queen Mine in the Mojave Desert was the source for many of the rocks (some with actual gold ore) lining the queue as well as a stamp mill that is over one hundred years old. Other artifacts were found in deserted mines in Wyoming, Nevada, Colorado and Minnesota.

63

An old mule trail still exists along the ridge separating Big Thunder Trail from the Rivers of America, where tourists once rode live animals.

The Pack Mule trail traced the length of the low foothills in Frontierland, off to the side of Tom Sawyer Island, and intertwined with the broader path used by the Disneyland Stagecoach. Today, glimpses of the Pack Mule trail are still possible from the bridge at one end of Big Thunder Trail.

FURTHERMORE: The ride had gone through a couple of name changes; it began as the Pack Mules, then became the Rainbow Ridge Pack Mules, and finally the Pack Mules Through Nature's Wonderland. What's left of the trail today travels only along the one ridge, from the former Cascade Peak over to the Indian Village.

64

The unusual rock sculpture along Big Thunder Trail was originally part of Mine Train Through Nature's Wonderland.

These buttes once marked the start of Balancing Rock Canyon in Nature's Wonderland, and were left standing for the Big Thunder Ranch area when the attraction closed. Designers preserved many other elements from the Nature's Wonderland area for use in the Big Thunder attraction in Florida as well, such as cacti and mountain sheep. Guests with long memories will also note that the dinosaur skeleton in the splashdown of today's Big Thunder Mountain Railroad are bones re-used from a skeleton in Nature's Wonderland; only the bones above riders' heads are new.

FURTHERMORE: Horseshoes nailed above the entrances to two tunnels in the ride provide some thematic clues for what lies ahead. As Guests enter the first tunnel that features bats and waterfalls, they may notice a horseshoe aligned right-side up at the start of the tunnel; this signifies good luck. However, the tunnel which houses the earthquake is heralded by an upside-down horseshoe – a harbinger of bad luck.

65

Some of the robotic animals from Mine Train Through Nature's Wonderland, a long-gone ride, still operate in Disneyland.

Near Big Thunder Mountain Railroad is a pond, and modern day visitors can still discern the "jumping fish" in that pond, which had been the bears' home in Nature's Wonderland. There are also marmots along the last remaining stretch of track in Nature's Wonderland which pop up from the ore gondolas behind the locomotive (itself an original relic from the attraction). These marmots were once positioned above the nearby tunnel still visible next to the French-fry cart in Frontierland.

FURTHERMORE: In 1997, a panther originally from the Mine Train attraction was added to the Disneyland Railroad. There had been 204 individually animated creatures in Nature's Wonderland, quite an impressive cast considering that the first official use of the more accomplished *Audio-Animatronics* wasn't until the Enchanted Tiki Room's opening three years later. Since designers didn't know what else to do with them, some of those mechanical creatures were simply buried under Big Thunder Ranch when the Mine Train Through Nature's Wonderland closed, and they are still there today.

Fantasyland

66

The sleigh benches on the Casey Jr. Circus Train came from the original Dentzel Merry-Go-Round purchased to create King Arthur Carrousel.

Because Walt wanted a carrousel – which by definition should only have horses – the stationary benches were removed, but they were put to good use as the basis for cars in the train. The Casey Jr. train is otherwise mostly composed of cages, since this is meant to represent a circus train.

FURTHERMORE: The Casey Jr. train was conceived as a theme park version of Walt's backyard miniature train, though on a slightly larger scale. The earliest plans for a park near the Disney studio included such a train intertwining with a gravity boat ride similarly themed in miniature. While the idea of miniatures in the eventual boat ride of Storybook Land has endured, the pint-sized train grew in scale when it became instead based on the circus train from *Dumbo* (1941).

67

An improperly placed exit sign at the Village Haus had to be "centered" by theming.

The Village Haus, newly constructed in 1983, was built without the required exit signs, so when these were added, designers found that one doorway left too little room for the sign. Forced to place it off-center, they compensated by painting Figaro the cat nearby, since Figaro and other characters adorned the walls of the restaurant anyway. But this Figaro held a rope, as if he were dragging the exit sign toward its normal centered position.

FURTHERMORE: Mindful of the slip-up in Anaheim, designers corrected the centering problem when a version of the Village Haus was built for Disneyland Paris in 1992. As an homage, however, a nearby Figaro was painted leaning against the now-centered exit sign, giving a thumbs-up.

68

The Snow White figure in her dark ride was not part of the attraction until it was rebuilt in 1982.

Originally, the heroes of the Disney stories did not appear in Fantasyland's dark rides: the characters of Peter Pan and Snow White were missing. The idea was that the Guests took the place of the characters, so it would make no sense to see the characters. To this day, Mr. Toad does not appear in his own attraction.

FURTHERMORE: Riders found the idea of supplanting the characters non-intuitive, and continually asked where Snow White and Peter Pan were, so these characters were added for the rehab. When Pinocchio was built in 1982-83, the main character was incorporated from the beginning. The nature of the Toad attraction makes it more obvious that the Guests are taking the place of the main character.

69

Elements of the large pirate ship in Peter Pan's Flight come from the Chicken of the Sea Pirate Ship in the outdoor Skull Rock Lagoon.

When the Pirate Ship and Skull Rock were demolished for the Fantasyland of 1983, some of the rigging on the ship as well as lanterns and props were brought into the Peter Pan attraction and used to bring more life into the pirate ship set piece. Disneyland Paris's version of the Pirate Ship at Skull Rock, built years later, used the original blueprints as a guide for construction.

FURTHERMORE: Peter Pan's Flight was originally designed as a roller-coaster. To convey a sense of being Peter Pan, who flies around quickly, Walt wanted the attraction to move fast along the ceiling; it would have been the world's first suspended roller-coaster. Similar plans for a coaster-like Toad would have simulated the helter-skelter pace of Toad's driving. In both cases, it was decided that such speeds would make the sets and characters pass by in a blur. Show, for Walt, would win out over thrills.

70

The King Arthur Carrousel rotates counter-clockwise to simulate jousting.

Most merry-go-rounds rotate in the other direction, but King Arthur Carrousel, which pointedly has only horses instead of the usual menagerie, turns counter-clockwise to give precedence to the right side – a necessary step to simulate jousting. The carrousel, a Dentzel model, was built by hand in 1922. All of its original horses were retained, and others, including some from Coney Island, were added to create an all-horse attraction.

FURTHERMORE: The carrousel's 85 unique horses are capped by one of special significance. The lead horse, always so named because the master carver spent extra time on it, is nicknamed Jingles on Disneyland's carrousel. Jingles is elaborately decorated with simulated bells and often used as a starting point for counting the horses when maintenance workers assign unique numbers to each horse.

71

Sleeping Beauty Castle is modeled after Neuschwanstein, a castle in Bavaria, Germany.

While the base of Sleeping Beauty Castle is not a copy of any one structure, the top parts are a proportional copy of the famous castle built by King Ludwig II. However, there is one crucial difference: Disneyland's castle is backwards. The "outside" of Neuschwanstein is actually the backside of Sleeping Beauty Castle.

FURTHERMORE: Walt made the decision himself regarding the castle's layout. The designers had argued about which way looked better – forwards or backwards – when Walt walked in the room. The top portion happened to be backwards at that moment, and he liked what he saw.

72

The Disney Family crest adorns the front of Sleeping Beauty Castle.

The coat-of-arms, with its triple set of lions surrounded by stylized flourishes, can be found right above the portcullis in the middle of the castle's drawbridge entrance. At Walt Disney World's Magic Kingdom, Cinderella Castle displays the same crest on the back side of the castle, as well as above a fireplace in the waiting room for the Cinderella's Royal Table, the restaurant inside the castle. While the crests were built with the castle at Walt Disney World, the one in Anaheim was not added until the 1960s.

FURTHERMORE: The drawbridge just below the crest at Sleeping Beauty Castle was once functional, though it was only lowered on two occasions: once during the grand opening in 1955, and a second time in 1983 when a renovated Fantasyland was rededicated. At the 1983 ceremony, two of the same children from the original dedication had been invited back, this time as adults, to again be the first to cross the drawbridge.

73

A plaque marks the spot where Disneyland buried a time capsule in front of the castle in 1995.

The capsule was sealed on Disneyland's 40th birthday and won't be unearthed until another 40 years have gone by. Several dozen items were packed into the capsule such as souvenir coins, watches, pins, buttons, photos, brochures, newspapers, press releases, Cast Member materials, and nametags, including a 1955 version belonging to Bob Penfield, who later became the last remaining original Disneyland Cast Member.

FURTHERMORE: An ornate capsule shaped like a castle was lowered into the ground, but it isn't the capsule currently buried; the day after the public ceremony, a plain container was substituted in the ground, and the "Time Castle" was sent into storage in a Disneyland warehouse. This was not the first "time capsule" at the park; one on a smaller scale was sealed under the manager's office of the redesigned Emporium in 1990, which in turn had been triggered by the discovery during the same refurbishment of a 1955 newspaper in the drywall of the Emporium, apparently also planted as a sort of time capsule.

74

A pine tree planted near Sleeping Beauty Castle honors Imagineer Herb Ryman.

One of the prime artists and designers of Disneyland, Herb had kept a dying tree near his bed as his health waned and joked that he'd try to live longer than the tree. When Herb died, the tree was brought to Disneyland and planted near the Snow White Wishing Well in his honor. The original Ryman tree has since died out, but each time the one planted in his honor dies, it is replaced by a new one.

FURTHERMORE: Another unheralded tree in Frontierland has an equally interesting history: the large tree in front of River Belle Terrace has a section of oil pipeline entangled in its root system. The rubber tree, a gift to Disneyland by a large oil company, had grown roots around a thin oil-carrying pipe in its original home. The pipeline was temporarily shut down to remove the tree, but the section of pipe could not be removed without destroying the root structure, so the pipe was left intact when the tree was relocated to Disneyland.

75

The figures at the Snow White Wishing Well are all the same size.

The statue of Snow White is placed at the top of the grotto to make her appear taller than she is, via a technique known as "forced perspective." The statues of Snow White and the seven dwarfs were rumored to be created in Italy by sculptor Leonida Parma and given to Walt as a gift, who promptly found a home for them in Disneyland. Early plans for a proto-Disneyland in Burbank – then called "Disneylandia" – also included a "singing waterfall," another idea that survived into the present-day Disneyland in the form of Snow White Grotto.

FURTHERMORE: Officials at the Oriental Land Company, which owns Tokyo Disneyland, insisted on a Snow White Grotto that resembled Disneyland's own down to the last detail. The oversight in sizing, once considered a shortcoming that needed to be overcome with forced perspective, had become part of the area's charm.

76

The giant mushroom at the loading zone of Alice in Wonderland is a former ticket booth.

In the days before "unlimited use" passports, Disneyland attractions were paid for by coupons, which had to be collected at each attraction. Whenever possible, themed booths were created for this purpose, but most have since been removed from the Park since they are no longer necessary. A close inspection of the mushroom reveals the outlines of the doorway in the structure, since the ticket-taker sat inside.

FURTHERMORE: The original ticket booth for Storybook Land, right across the way, is also still present in the form of the narrow Lighthouse along the sidewalk, though its previous location was closer to Monstro. Thus, two of the only few remaining ticket booths at Disneyland are right next to each other. The colorful shack next to the Casey Jr. Circus train is a third original ticket booth, and a fourth – once used centrally in the original Fantasyland – now is home to the Kodak kiosk in Small World Way. Tickets for the Matterhorn were once distributed in the window between the two turnstiles.

77

The Matterhorn attraction was partially inspired by a pile of dirt left over from construction of the Park.

The area between Tomorrowland and Fantasyland that would later be used for the Motor Boat Cruise and the Fantasyland Autopia was originally cleared for an area known as "Holidayland." The dirt moved for Holidayland had been piled up in a mound and used as a base for one of the pylons used for the sky ride.

FURTHERMORE: Walt had been looking at Holiday Hill, as it was originally called, and thinking about the filming of *Third Man on the Mountain* on the real Matterhorn mountain in Switzerland, when inspiration struck to build his own Matterhorn on the location of this semi-mountainous pile of dirt. Holiday Hill quickly became "Snow Hill" to enthusiastic Cast Members who heard about Walt's idea for a toboggan ride.

78

Gaping holes in the sides of the Matterhorn give testament to the now-removed Skyway ride.

Though these holes are now partly filled in with faux stalagmites and stalactites, their general outlines are still visible on both the Tomorrowland and Fantasyland sides. The Skyway attraction once bisected the Matterhorn, offering one-way rides in both directions as a quick way to cross the park. One of the stalagmites in the cave on the Fantasyland side was crafted intentionally to look like a handle, because designers thought the hole had been teacup-shaped. The Mad Tea Party's proximity below only added to the synergy of recognizing the teacup shape in the mountain.

FURTHERMORE: Designers had to plan the Matterhorn so that the Skyway lines would again be hung at the exact point in space after the mountain was built. Though the lines were temporarily removed during construction, the Matterhorn was essentially built around the Skyway.

79

Trees along the sides of the Matterhorn are given limited soil to stunt their growth.

Because the coaster was essentially a scaled version of a mountain, truly unusual construction techniques and set designs were required. The steel superstructure, for example, called for thousands of steel bars of different length; in fact, no two were alike. Outside the mountain, designers had to decide the nonintuitive question of where the timberline should be. Colorado spruce trees and pinion pines from mountainous regions in Arizona were purchased for areas high on the Matterhorn, and kept stunted by limiting their soil and thus their root structure.

FURTHERMORE: The Matterhorn was the world's first steel tubular roller-coaster. Steel coasters had existed before, but they had flat steel tracks rather than a tube, as virtually all steel coasters have today. In essence, almost all modern steel coasters are descendants of the Matterhorn. It was designed and built with help from Arrow Dynamics, a coaster company that has since become one of the world's largest. Due to its unique design, a special oil lubricant had to be created for it called the "Matterhorn Special" — it was made just for Disneyland.

80

Former Walt Disney Company President Frank Wells is honored in the Matterhorn.

Wells, who with CEO Michael Eisner turned the company around in 1984 and sparked its creative revival, was an avid mountain climber. After Wells died on Easter Sunday, 1994, in a helicopter crash while on a skiing trip, Disneyland honored him by creating a "Wells Expedition" memorial near the beginning of the attraction. Wells also has a window on Main Street, U.S.A., above the bank. The inscription reads: "Seven Summits Expeditions – Frank G. Wells – President."

FURTHERMORE: One unheralded invention used at the Matterhorn called "booster brakes" assisted in the creation of the PeopleMover. The brakes are actually tires embedded in the track, which slow bobsleds as they pass by. Seeing this, Walt reckoned that powered wheels in the track could be used to do the reverse; to power a vehicle forward. This idea was born while Walt watched steel blocks being moved around on conveyer belts at the Ford factory, and he realized that wheels on a continuous conveyer-belt type system would work wonderfully as a way to move people. Several years later, the PeopleMover concept made use of this powered tire technology.

81

Storybook Land is divided into countries to match its original theme of "Canal Boats of the World."

When Storybook Land opened, there were attempts on promotional artwork to bridge its new theme with its old international one by creating divisions in the Storybook lands that corresponded to countries: Italy for Geppetto's Village, England for Alice and Mr. Toad, Germany for Snow White, France for Cinderella, and Holland for the Old Mill. Thus Storybook is still, in a way, a journey on Canal Boats of the World.

FURTHERMORE: The miniaturized scale of Storybook Land can be traced to Walt's initial idea of a Lilliputian Land in this space, themed to *Gulliver's Travels*. Limited technology preventing the building of a Lilliputian Land, and the ride was eventually opened as Canal Boats of the World. Despite such a fancy name, there was little to look at along the banks of the attraction, and extensive revisions led to a thematic change as well when the ride re-opened as Storybook Land. The scale of Storybook Land is one of the smallest in Disneyland at one-twelfth (one inch to a foot).

82

The Storybook Land Canal Boats marks the start of the giant interconnected "dark water" system at Disneyland.

While attractions that use clear water are self-contained, many attractions that use dyed, murky water share the same water system. From the Storybook Land Canal Boats, water flows underground via gravity (the Disneyland site was once a natural riverbed) to the Motor Boat Lagoon, the Matterhorn, and on to the Sleeping Beauty Castle moat, Jungle Cruise, Tarzan's Treehouse, and the Rivers of America, where it is pumped back up to Storybook Land.

FURTHERMORE: The only visible portion of the water system in transit is a stream running from the Castle, alongside the Tiki Room, and over to the Jungle Cruise. Before New Orleans Square was built, Guests could cross a bridge between Adventureland and Frontierland, under which the water flowed plainly into the Rivers of America. This passageway is now underground and hidden.

83

The bronzed decorations atop the spires of "it's a small world" are exact copies of Imagineer Leota Thomas' jewelry.

The designer was at the time working on the attraction, and her sometimes fantastical earrings, pendants, and charms provided a sudden inspiration for the tops of the spires. The designs of her jewelry were simply copied and produced on a much larger scale for the attraction's façade.

FURTHERMORE: When creating the original show, Walt at first wanted the dolls to sing their own national anthems, but the various musical styles did not mesh together well, so he turned to songwriters Richard and Robert Sherman for a catchy tune that could be sung in different languages. In the holiday overlay, dolls normally alternate between "Jingle Bells" and the theme song, although mermaids in "it's a small world holiday" sing "Jingle Shells." "it's a small world holiday" concludes with "Deck the Halls," a song that captures the universalizing message of the attraction: national and racial differences melt away, replaced with a message of peace on earth – which is pretty close to Walt's intention when creating the ride.

84

One doll in "it's a small world" pays homage to the attraction's primary designer Mary Blair.

Since she was frequently seen wearing a poncho, black tights, black turtleneck, and boots, Blair was honored in the France section by a similarly attired doll. Her tribute doll can be seen halfway up the miniature Eiffel Tower in the ride.

FURTHERMORE: There are trees atop the attraction building because of Walt's unexpected visit to the designers. The attraction, when it was moved to Disneyland after the 1964-1965 World's Fair, retained the same show, meaning that only countries which were members of UNICEF were represented in the show. Indeed, the Pepsi-sponsored show was subtitled "A Salute to UNICEF." But the ride would require a new show building, and designers were working on the scale model when Walt walked in to visit them. They had temporarily placed a couple of model trees on the building's roof just to keep them within arm's reach, but Walt took the placement seriously and liked the idea, since it would generate the impression from the front that there is no building behind the façade. To this day, the trees remain atop the roof of the building.

Mickey's Toontown

85

One of the pumpkins outside Goofy's Bounce House pays homage to a former Disneyland official.

Jack Lindquist, Disneyland's top official from 1990-1993, presided over the opening of Mickey's Toontown as his crowning achievement. To commemorate him, designers crafted a pumpkin in his likeness, an idea inspired by a pumpkin patch outside Goofy's Bounce House, where pumpkins already had cartoonish faces on them. There had been multiple ideas for a tribute to Jack, including plastering his name as "Toontown Postmaster" on an interactive mailbox, or creating a crazy golf calendar to hang in Goofy's Bounce House, since Jack was an avid golfer. Imagineering director Marty Sklar chose the winning design.

FURTHERMORE: Imagineers also sprinkled inside jokes elsewhere in the land. The blueprint hanging in the Gadget's Go Coaster load zone refers to the device's machine parts by strange names – these are in fact the last names of the Imagineeers on the project. One of the show set designers for Minnie's house was crazy about Elvis, so she snuck in a book titled "Elvis: What Happened" into Minnie's kitchen. In Mickey's house, a calendar near the washing machine had to be created without reference to a specific month, but that designer added character to it by circling his own birthday.

86

Toontown's Fireworks Factory uses a theme created for a land never built.

A new land along Big Thunder Trail called Discovery Bay would have bridged Frontierland and Fantasyland. Set as a western port in Gold Rush-era San Francisco, the land was to focus on discovery and invention, and include attractions on Captain Nemo, magnetism, time travel, and airships. The land would have also featured a Chinatown and a shooting gallery named the Fireworks Factory.

FURTHERMORE: The connection between fireworks and Chinatown lives on today in a mural between Stagedoor Café and the River Belle Terrace, which advertises "Laod Bhang & Co. Fireworks Rocket Factory." The Laod Bhang billboard, in turn, inspired the theming of a pin trading cart in Disney's California Adventure.

87

The cow patterns on the windows of Clarabelle's Frozen Yogurt form a "Hidden Mickey."

Hidden Mickeys are sprinkled throughout Disneyland in both subtle and obvious ways. Many newer locations feature hidden or obscure Mickey Mouse shapes to appeal to Guests with sharp eyes and also to reinforce the idea that this is Mickey's Park.

FURTHERMORE: The first intentional Hidden Mickeys are thought to be the giant water molecules from Adventure Thru Inner Space: the small hydrogen atoms sitting atop the larger oxygen atoms were apparently deliberate references to the Mickey shape. Other references followed in later attractions, shops, and restaurants, and such Hidden Mickeys are now included on many new construction projects.

88

Walt Disney has no window on Main Street, but he does have one in Mickey's Toontown.

The text of the window above the Toontown Library in the Civic Center pays homage to Walt and his first commercial success: the Laugh-O-Gram short cartoons that first brought riches and fame to the young Walt, long before Mickey Mouse was created.

FURTHERMORE: Though Walt did not install a window honoring himself during his lifetime, he made certain that his father Elias did have a window on Main Street. Elias is listed above the Emporium as a contractor, which indeed he was. There is also a Hotel Marceline on Main Street, honoring the small town in Missouri where Walt spent his pivotal formative years.

Tomorrowland

89

Edible agriculture in Tomorrowland was added intentionally to support Tomorrowland's theme of integrating greenery and urban space.

Termed "Agrifuture" by designers, the mixing of urban structures and lush flora aims to inspire a future where cities are not separate from nature. The word "Agrifuture" can even be seen on a billboard from the Disneyland Railroad. Like the cacti of Frontierland and the palms of Adventureland, "the edible Garden of Eden" was an attempt to define the land through its landscape.

FURTHERMORE: Competing ideas for a late 1990s Tomorrowland upgrade included the "Montana Future," which also combined cities with vegetation in the form of thickly forested areas, and so enraptured sponsor General Motors that they designed a "Montana Minivan" around the concept. Another idea was "Tomorrowland 2055," which called for a gleaming, domed city of steel and chrome. The "Tomorrowland 2055" vision would maintain a digital, futuristic look one expects from science fiction. In that vision, the Carousel building would have housed Plectu's Fantastic Galactic Revue, an outer-space musical revue put on by aliens, which was to replicate the basic show structure of America Sings. Plectu was partly an outgrowth of an interim idea called Robot Show, which mimicked the industrial robot shows at Epcot's Communicore and World of Motion.

90

The Astro Orbitor's kinetic top improved upon a similar attraction at Disneyland Paris.

The upper portion of the Astro Orbitor in Paris, which predated the Anaheim version, had been faulty. A new but similar design was tested at Disneyland, and then a duplicate was created for Paris. This was not the first time Disneyland had exchanged ideas or even parts with its European cousin. The entire Dumbo attraction presently installed at Disneyland had been built for the grand opening of Euro Disneyland (as it was then known), but was installed on an emergency basis at Disneyland instead, and a second was created for Paris. The figures in the Well Scene at the Pirates of the Caribbean being readied for Paris were similarly purchased by Disneyland during a 14-week refurbishment in 1990.

FURTHERMORE: The Astro Orbitor's sculpture, which resembles a three-dimensional model of a solar system, was inspired by Leonardo da Vinci's astrolabe sketch and designed after medieval models of the solar system. The cosmic connection ties back to the Astro Orbitor's name; Guests are in space (the astros), orbiting around a solar system.

91

A 1960s-era tile mural by artist Mary Blair is still hidden underneath the Star Tours and Transportation murals in Tomorrowland.

Mary's tile murals of happy children – symbolic of an optimistic future – were covered up on one side of the land by a Star Tours mural in 1987, and on the other side in 1998 by a historical mural displaying the various modes of transportation in Tomorrowland. Blair's tiles still exist partly intact, though heavily cracked, beneath both murals. Portions of the tiles destroyed by the new mural attachments were fashioned into an abstract mosiac outside a restaurant at Disneyland Paris. Similar tile murals by Blair can still be seen at Walt Disney World's Contemporary Resort.

FURTHERMORE: The newest Tomorrowland mural traces the history of transportation in Tomorrowland, and nods to its own past by portraying stylized versions of such historical vehicles as the Viewliner, Flying Saucers, bubble-topped Monorails, and Submarines. The Blair murals had also been organized thematically, covering renewable energy sources (on the Monsanto/Star Tours side) and communication (on the Circle-Vision/Buzz Lightyear side).

92

The G2 repair droid in the Star Tours queue is a former goose from America Sings.

Savvy visitors can detect the webbed feet and wagging tail of the droid, which was removed from the America Sings attraction in 1986. A second goose was used in the Star Tours queue as a kind of intergalactic dispatcher. After the geese were removed from America Sings, the show continued operating for a few years. Most of the rest of the America Sings cast was later used in Splash Mountain. The hens in Splash Mountain's riverboat finale have outstretched arms because they were crafted to sing gospel music in America Sings.

FURTHERMORE: Unlike the repair droids in the queue, the droids piloting the Starspeeders were newly created for the attraction. Our pilot Rex, in fact, is meant to represent a brand new, untested pilot with poor training. There is even packing tape attached to the droid which reads "Remove before flight."

93

A prop from Adventure Thru Inner Space is visible in the Star Tours movie.

Adventure Thru Inner Space, which resided in the same building before Star Tours, sported a "Mighty Microscope" in its queue. In the Star Tours movie, this Microscope is visible along the bottom of the screen on the right side, as our Starspeeder zooms out of the hangar. Guests can even see the miniaturized Atomobiles still in the top of the Microscope as they zoom by. There are two other tributes: one of those tiny Atomobiles from the Microscope moves around in the "spare parts" conveyer system overhead in the second Star Tours queue area, and one of the consoles worked on by a R2 droid at the bottom queue level was formerly a display box from the Inner Space queue.

FURTHERMORE: The R2-D2 and C-3PO droids seen in the queue are actual movie props from the original trilogy. C-3PO, in fact, is overlaid with real gold so that the robot wouldn't rust during filming. Inside the Starspeeders, Paul Reubens provides the voice of Captain Rex. Reubens, best known for the character of "Pee-wee" Herman, is uncredited in the role, so his voice isn't immediately apparent to many Guests, at least until he yelps his characteristic laugh.

94

Footage from Mission to Mars was used in the old Space Mountain queue video.

The downward view of a rocket ship blasting off came from the floor viewscreen in the old Tomorrowland attraction Mission to Mars (and before that, from Flight to the Moon). This film played during the "Space Mountain Mission Control" sequence in the queue video. Another Mission Control sequence showed a satellite unfurling its solar panels, which formed into the familiar Mickey Mouse shape.

FURTHERMORE: The Mickey satellite was part of a stop-motion animation done years earlier for the launch of the Disney Channel. The video loop as a whole was meant to represent channel surfing through "Space Mountain TV." There were cameos by actors Charles Fleischer (the voice of Roger Rabbit) as Crazy Larry, Kelly Coffield (from *In Living Color*) as the weather girl, and Glenn Shadix (the voice of the Mayor from *The Nightmare Before Christmas*) as the intergalactic fashion consultant Ray Cathode.

95

The rocket launch in Space Mountain's old soundtrack was inspired by the Batman TV series.

The Disney Imagineer in charge hit upon two ideas for Space Mountain's soundtrack by examining his own driving habits. He would start his car while thinking of the Batmobile from the 1960s series, where a rocket roar accompanies dialogue stating "we have ignition." Then, once he reached cruising speed, he'd listen to Dick Dale's surf guitar music as he roared down the street. Both features became part of the Space Mountain soundtrack.

FURTHERMORE: The opening and closing segments of the soundtrack were adaptations of "Aquarium" from classical composer Saint Saëns' "Carnevale des Animaux." The idea to synchronize music to an indoor roller coaster was first realized in Space Mountain at Disneyland Paris, which used an original score created just for that attraction. Part of that score can be heard at the Observatron.

96

Part of the exterior of Innoventions pays tribute to the all-plastic House of the Future.

The Monsanto-sponsored plastic house was formerly located in Triton Gardens, between Tomorrowland and Sleeping Beauty Castle. Several paintings of the House's distinctive shape adorn the exterior of Innoventions' Home Zone, and the house is also shown briefly in the introductory video with Tom Morrow.

FURTHERMORE: The House was so sturdy, a wrecking ball could not demolish it when it had finally grown outdated. The wrecking ball just bounced off the tough, futuristic plastic. Choker cables had to be used to separate the big plastic modules into pieces small enough to be trucked away. Monsanto, sponsor of the House, took pride in the fact that even then it wasn't the plastic which broke; it was the steel bolts that broke and allowed dismantling.

97

The song sung by the robotic host of Innoventions pays homage to Carousel of Progress, the first attraction in this building.

The original occupant of the present-day Innoventions building, the Carousel of Progress, followed a family and its technology at home through several 20th century decades. The song currently performed by the welcoming robot Tom Morrow is called "Great Big World of Innoventions," which borrows both the tune and the majority of the words from the original theme song in the Carousel of Progress, "There's a Great Big Beautiful Tomorrow." When Innoventions opened, numerous pictures of the *Audio-Animatronics* family were also hung along the sets in the outer ring as a tribute.

FURTHERMORE: The Sherman Brothers, creators of many songs for both Disneyland and Disney movies such as *Mary Poppins*, composed "Great Big World of Innoventions" as well as the original theme song from the Carousel of Progress. The Sherman brothers also created songs for "it's a small world" and the Enchanted Tiki Room, and instrumental versions of their songs can be heard at Big Thunder Mountain Railroad, the Disney Gallery, King Arthur Carrousel, and Main Street, U.S.A..

98

Innoventions' host Tom Morrow has a long tradition in Tomorrowland.

He first appeared in Flight to the Moon as the flight control commander, though he was later renamed Mr. Johnson when the attraction was changed in 1975 to Mission to Mars. His name is also mentioned in the Star Tours queue during the terminal announcements: "Mr. Morrow, Mr. Tom Morrow, please check with a Star Tours agent at gate number four."

FURTHERMORE: The same terminal announcement references George Lucas by saying his name backwards: "Departing Endor passenger, Sacul; Mr. Egroeg Sacul, please see the Star Tours agent at gate number three." Lucas' first film, *THX1138*, is also mentioned as the license number of a landspeeder "parked in a no-hover zone."

99

A "Fun Phone" outside Innoventions references Adventure Thru Inner Space.

The recording which plays when Guests pick up the phone mimics the opening lines of Adventure Thru Inner Space, a former Tomorrowland attraction, but changes the original mentions of sight and vision into auditory associations: "For centuries, man had but his own two ears to explore the wonders of his world. Then he invented the telephone, a Mighty Ear. Now your adventure through telecommunications is about to begin."

FURTHERMORE: A similar phone outside the Indiana Jones Adventure mentions, via several different recordings, such Adventureland references as Trader Sam, the Chamber of Earthly Riches, Schweitzer Falls, and even the Swiss Family Robinson (which the operator humorously cannot seem to locate, since Tarzan has taken over their former treehouse home).

100

The base of an unused pylon in the middle of the Autopia marks the original track layout for the monorail.

The monorail used to leave its station and immediately turn left, in the days before its track was altered to go to the Disneyland Hotel. The base of this first pylon left over from the old track is still there in the Autopia area – it's just a rectangular concrete stump painted over.

FURTHERMORE: The last curve around the Matterhorn for the monorail track used to be different as well. The curve formerly ended in an S-turn into the station. When the monorail underwent upgrades, the train was lengthened and it couldn't negotiate this S-turn any more, so designers had to straighten the track so that the train would be able to pull into the station.

101

The bronzed miniature car along the Autopia track is a relic from an earlier Disneyland attraction.

The vehicle came from the Midget Autopia, an attraction in Fantasyland for very young children from 1957-1966. In 1966, Walt donated the Midget Autopia to his "home town" of Marceline, Missouri, and designers headed there when refurbishing the attraction in 2000 to find the old attraction. They arranged to borrow one vehicle, and returned it to Disneyland in a place of honor beside the new Autopia.

FURTHERMORE: The redesigned Autopia cars now include different car types: Guests might ride in Sparky (a sports car), Suzy (a convertible), Dusty (an SUV), or Classic (which approximates the original Autopia designs). The cars come in 12 colors, including one called "chromalusion," which changes color depending upon the angle at which it's viewed. Created by DuPont, chromalusion uses a colorless material that forms a flake in five layers, which together are only 1/50th the width of a human hair. Light entering the flake reflects wavelengths of light back that vary depending on thickness, generating many different colors.

Coda: It's a Small World, After All
(Or, Six Degrees of Disneyland Designers)

- **The 1984 Olympics Ceremonies in Los Angeles were in multiple ways Disney-produced affairs.**
  Imagineer Bob Gurr created the flying saucer that closed the 1984 Olympics, while the "Rocket Man" from that Olympics is the same person who used to perform in Tomorrowland – a man named William P. Suitor. To top it all off, Disney artists created Sam the Olympic Eagle, used as the Games' symbol in 1984.

- **Michael Jackson can be connected not only to Tomorrowland, but also Main Street, U.S.A.**
  Michael, the former Captain EO, had an on-screen presence in Tomorrowland for years. He was born in Gary, Indiana, which is the name of a song that plays on the Main Street music loop. If Michael is aware of the movie *The Music Man*, from which the Disneyland track is taken, he must surely recognize the tune named after his hometown.

- **The two dioramas along the Disneyland Railroad can be indirectly linked by their content.**
  "The Grand Canyon Suite," composed by Ferde Grofé, plays in the Grand Canyon Diorama. Grofé also

composed the "Niagara Falls Suite," which was created to commemorate the opening of the Robert Moses Power Plant in New York. Robert Moses, meanwhile, was the mastermind of the 1964-65 New York World's Fair, which is where the Primeval World debuted, as part of Ford's Magic Highway.

- **Disney artist Peter Ellenshaw worked on many areas of Disneyland. But the Ellenshaw heritage extends beyond just Peter's work.**

  Peter's son Harrison worked on *Tron* (later to be seen in part with the PeopleMover), on Captain EO, which showed for years in Tomorrowland, and on the *Star Wars* movies, which are represented by Star Tours.

Postscript: Untrue Urban Legends

- **One spire atop Sleeping Beauty Castle supposedly remains ungilded as a physical manifestation of Walt's creedo that "Disneyland will never be completed."**
  When the castle was redesigned in the 1990s, the spire atop the chapel was covered with patina bronze and gold decoration rather than gilded by gold leaf like the others. The idea was to make it stand out – just because it looked good – but designers later admitted the different design simply makes it look like it had been forgotten.

- **The bronze spike underneath Sleeping Beauty Castle allegedly marks the exact center of Disneyland in 1955.**
  In fact, the center of Disneyland upon its opening (in the days before Mickey's Toontown) was at the Hub, or Central Plaza. This was part of the idea behind Walt's notion that museums and traditional amusement parks were laid out poorly – with the Central Plaza, visitors could quickly and easily traverse to another section of the park. The bronze spike underneath the castle was simply one of many survey markers throughout Disneyland, in this case marking the centerline of Main

Street through the castle. Builders had to be sure the castle was centered when viewed from Main Street.

- **The hearse outside the Haunted Mansion is sometimes said to have carried Brigham Young to his grave.**
  While the hearse is irrefutably old and authentic, representatives of the Mormon Church claim that no hearse at all was used at Brigham Young's funeral, pointing to conclusive historical documents, including Young's will.

- **One horse in King Arthur's Carrousel had its tooth painted gold supposedly so that Walt's wife Lillian could find her favorite horse.**
  The horse with the golden tooth certainly exists, but neither the designers from the ride's last two major refurbishments (including Imagineer John Hench, who helped design and build Disneyland) nor the Walt Disney Archives are able to establish any truth to the rumor that the tooth was so painted for Lillian.

- **The "Hidden Mickey" in a cow pattern on Clarabelle's supposedly pays homage to Mickey Moo.**
  Disneyland's milk cow from the 80s and 90s, Mickey Moo, was so named for her distinctive Mickey Mouse pattern on one side. A similarly patterned shutter on Clarabelle's Frozen Yogurt often leads to speculation that

the Hidden Mickey was an homage to Mickey Moo, but Toontown designers chalk the cow-mouse connection up to coincidence, though they admit the intentional Hidden Mickey.

- **Many believe Disneyland was built on a scale of 5/8th.**
  While the steam trains and the Mark Twain's lower deck are a 5/8th's scale, this represented no magical number for the entire park. Main Street's shops are built at 90% of full size on the first floor, and 80% on the second floor. The Matterhorn is 1/100th scale, and the models in Storybook Land are 1/12th – one inch to a foot. Designers simply eyeball each new addition, and use whatever scale looks good on a given project.

Afterword

Disneyland is magic.

Disneyland is in the business of creating happiness, which really means creating happy experiences and lasting memories. While any amusement park can deliver thrills, chills and excitement, sometimes even in a themed environment, Disneyland stands alone in crafting a rich atmosphere bursting with details.

A careful observer will note that those details aren't random; frequently, they bubble over with nostalgia, inside jokes, hidden meanings and homages to Disneyland's own past. These aren't just themed details, they are details with very specific meanings.

Disneyland isn't an "amusement park." It's a rich canvas, painted over many times but always with reverence and respect of its origins. At each reconception, the Park looks back to its past to give meaning to its future, and uses the "Disney Touch" of meaningful details to convey this continuum to the visitors. The magic is frequently said to be in the details, but sometimes, it's the details themselves which are magical. We hope this tour of the magical details has been as interesting for you as it was for us.

Kevin Yee
Jason Schultz

About the Authors

Kevin Yee, a Disney fan from birth, spent the better part of a decade working at Disneyland and cultivating a never-ending fascination with the Park's rich traditions and history. Now an academic on the East Coast, Kevin never lets his thoughts wander far from Walt's favorite creation in Anaheim.

Jason Schultz, a lifelong fan of the original Disneyland, can distinctly remember the day in 1995 when he became interested in knowing more about the Park's history and the resulting years of research and fun that led to the book before you. No doubt, his hunger for all things Disneyland will not abate.

Kevin and Jason also collaborated on a book called *Magic Quizdom: Disneylandia Minutiae Semper Absurda*, which is a trivia book focused only on Disneyland, and which features answers detailed enough to satisfy the trivia cravings from casual fans and hardcore Disney addicts alike. Their work can be ordered online at www.smalloaktree.com.